PAWSITIVELY PU...
CAT JOKES

Hallo

230+ CAT JOKES – PURRFECT FOR THE ENTIRE FAMILY!

PAWSITIVELY PURFECT CAT JOKES!

HEIDI BEE

DEDICATED TO ALL THE NAUGHTY CATS OUT THERE!

(ESPECIALLY RUFFI- TUFFI)

WELCOME!

CATS, WHAT WOULD THE WORLD BE WITHOUT THEM? SURE, MICE WOULD PROBABLY FEEL SAFER, AND YOU WOULD BE ABLE TO LEAVE YOUR GLASS SITTING SAFELY ON THE EDGE OF A BENCH AND NOT WORRY ABOUT IT GETTING KNOCKED OVER.

BUT A WORLD WITHOUT CATS IS SURELY A WORLD WITHOUT JOY, AND THIS BOOK SEEKS TO SPREAD A LITTLE BIT OF THE HUMOR AND LAUGHTER THAT CATS BRING INTO EVERY HOME - AND BOOKCASE!

PACKED TO THE BRIM WITH OVER 200 CAT JOKES AND PUNS, THIS BOOK IS FANTASTIC FOR CAT LOVERS OF ALL AGES, AND IS SO PURRFECT THAT EVEN DOGS WILL LAUGH OUT LOUD AS WELL!

HOW TO PLAY!

IT'S EASY TO PLAY ALONG!

IF YOU ARE READING THIS BOOK WITH FRIENDS OR FAMILY, ONE PERSON CAN READ THE FIRST PART OF THE JOKE WHILE EVERYONE ELSE TRIES TO GUESS THE CORRECT ANSWER. THE PERSON WHO IS CLOSEST WINS!

HOWEVER, THIS BOOK IS JUST AS FUN TO READ ON YOUR OWN! HOW MANY OF THE PUNS AND JOKES CAN YOU **FIGURE** OUT BEFORE THE ANSWER IS REVEALED?

REMEMBER, EVEN IF YOUR ANSWER IS DIFFERENT FROM THE ONE GIVEN, ALL CATS KNOW THAT THEY ARE ALWAYS RIGHT - AND SO ARE YOU! AS LONG AS YOU HAVE FURRN THAT IS ALL THAT MATTERS.

CHAPTER 1: TAILS AS OLD AS TIME

WHY DID THE CAT GO TO PRISON?

BECAUSE HE WAS CAUGHT LITTER-ING!

WHAT ANIMAL HAS MORE LIVES THAN A CAT?

A FROG - BECAUSE IT CROAKS EVERY NIGHT!

WHY ARE CATS BAD AT TELLING STORIES?

THEY ONLY HAVE 1 TAIL!

WHAT TYPE OF CAR DO CATS DRIVE?

A FURRARI!

WHAT ARE OLD CATS CALLED?

GRAND-PAW!

WHAT DO POOR CATS SADLY SAY?

I AM PAW!

WHAT ARE THE CAT POLICE CALLED?

THE CLAW ENFORCEMENT!

WHAT DO YOU CALL A CAT TANTRUM?

A HISSY-FIT!

WHEN WILL MY CAT RETURN HOME?

ANY MINUTE MEOW...

WHAT DO CATS EAT FOR BREAKFAST?

MICE KRISPIES!

WHY WAS THE CAT SO SMALL?

HE ONLY DRANK CONDENSED MILK!

WHAT DO YOU CALL A CAT WHO GIVES UP?

A QUITTY!

WHAT DO CATS WEAR TO BED?

PAW-JAMAS!

WHAT PIECE OF ART DO CATS
LOVE THE MOST?

THE PAW-TRAIT OF MEOWNA
LISA!

WHAT DO YOU CALL A CAT WHO
LIKES TO WEAR SHOES?

PUSS-IN-BOOTS!

WHY WAS THE CAT ANGRY?

HE WAS IN A BAD
MEWD!

WHAT VEGETABLE DO CATS LOVE THE MOST?

AS-PURR-AGUS!

WHAT MONUMENT DO CATS LOVE TO VISIT?

THE PURR-AMIDS OF GIZA!

WHY DID THE KITTEN GIVE HERSELF UP?

SHE WAS SICK OF PLAYING CAT AND MOUSE!

WHAT STATE IN THE US DO CATS LIKE TO VISIT?

CONNECTI-CAT!

WHY DID THE CAT GO TO JAIL?

PAW-SESSION OF CATNIP!

WHAT BOARD GAME DO CATS LIKE TO PLAY?

MOUSE TRAP!

WHAT SUBJECT DO CATS EXCEL AT IN SCHOOL?

HISS-TORY!

HOW DO YOU MAKE A CAT HAPPY?
SEND THEM TO THE CANARY ISLANDS!

WHAT DO YOU CALL A CAT'S HOUSE?

A SCRATCH PAD!

WHERE DOES A CAT KEEP HER COINS?

IN HER PURR-SE!

WHAT DO YOU CALL A LAZY CAT?

A PRO-CAT-STINATOR!

HOW DO CATS SING SCALES?

DO-RE-MEW!

DON'T FUR-GET TO BUY MORE CATNIP.

WHY WOULDN'T THE CAT STOP MEOWING?

HE DIDN'T WANT TO BE FURR-GOTTEN!

WHY DID NO-ONE TAKE THE CAT SERIOUSLY?

BECAUSE HE WAS ALWAYS KITTEN!

WHAT DO CATS THINK OF PUNS?

CLAWFUL!

WHICH TOM HANKS CHARACTER
DO CATS LOVE?

FURR-EST GUMP!

WHICH BOOK DO ALL CATS READ?

THE GREAT CATSBY!

WHAT DO CATS WEAR WHEN THEY
WANT TO SMELL GOOD?

PURR-FUME!

WHAT WEAPON DO CATS USE IN WARS?

CAT-APULTS!

HOW DO CATS MAKE COFFEE?

WITH A PURR-CULATOR!

WHY DID THE CATS ASK FOR A DRUM SET?

THEY WANTED TO MAKE SOME MEWSIC!

I'M A GLAMOUR-PUSS.

WHAT HORROR MOVIE DID CATS
SEE IN THEATRE?

THE PURRGE!

WHICH TV DRAMA DO CATS
WATCH?

CLAW AND ORDER!

WHAT DO CATS SAY AFTER
MAKING A JOKE?

JUST KITTEN!

WHAT IS A CAT'S FAVORITE DEAL?

BUY ONE, GET ONE FURRY!

WHO DO CATS CALL WHEN THEY NEED TO GO SOMEWHERE?

A TABBY!

WHY DO CATS MAKE GREAT BOSSES?

THEY HAVE GREAT LITTERSHIP!

WHAT DO CATS SAY WHEN SOMETHING BAD HAPPENS?

THAT'S UN-FUR-TUNATE!

WHY DID THE CAT NEED AN ACCOUNTANT?

BECAUSE THEY GOT CAUGHT UP IN A PURRAMID SCHEME!

WHAT IS IT CALLED WHEN ALL THE TREATS ARE GONE?

A CAT-ASTROPHE!

WHAT KIND OF CAT WORKS AT
THE RED CROSS?

A FIRST-AID KIT!

WHAT DO YOU CALL A STYLISH
CAT?

HAUTE-CAT-TURE!

WHAT DID THE KITTEN HAVE AT
THEIR PARTY?

A POUNCE HOUSE!

WHAT DO CATS SAY WHEN YOU STEP ON THEIR TAILS?

ME-OW!

WHY DO CATS GO TO SCHOOL?

TO BECOME LITTER-ATE!

HOW DOES A CAT SAY GOODBYE?

SEE YOU LITTER!

WHAT WAS THE KITTEN BOWLING
LEAGUE CALLED?

ALLEY CATS!

WHAT COLOR DO CATS LOVE?

YELLOW!

WHAT DO CATS LOOK FOR IN THEIR FRIENDS?

A GREAT PURR-SONALITY!

WHY DID THE CAT AVOID EATING LEMONS?

THEY MADE HIM A SOUR PUSS!

WHY DID THE CAT FAIL THEIR COMPUTER EXAM?

THEY KEPT TRYING TO EAT THE MOUSE!

WHAT SONG DO CATS DANCE TO?

MICE MICE BABY!

WHY DO CATS HATE LAPTOPS?

THEY DON'T HAVE A MOUSE!

WHAT TYPES OF PAINTINGS DO CATS LIKE BEST?

SELF PAW-TRAITS!

HOW DID ONE CAT BREAK UP WITH HER BOYFRIEND?

SHE SAID: WE'RE HISSTORY!!

WHY DON'T CATS SAY YOLO?

THEY HAVE 9 LIVES!

TAKE MEOWT FOR LUNCH.

WHAT DAY OF THE WEEK DO CATS LIKE BEST?

CATURDAY!

WHY ARE CATS POOR DJS?
THEY ALWAYS PAWS THE TUNES!

WHAT DO CATS CALL A NICE DINNER?

FANCY FEAST!

WHY DID THE CAT GET SENT TO DETENTION?

SHE HAD A BAD CATTATUDE!

WHAT DID THE SICK CAT SAY?
I FEEL CLAWFUL!

WHAT TYPE OF STICKERS DO CATS LOVE?

SCRATCH AND SNIFF!

WHAT DO YOU CALL A CAT WITH EIGHT LEGS?

AN OCTO-PUSS!

WHY ARE CATS SO GOOD AT VIDEO GAMES?

BECAUSE THEY HAVE 9 LIVES!

WHERE DO FRENCH CATS LIVE?

IN PURR-IS!

WHAT DO YOU FEED AN INVISIBLE CAT?

EVAPORATED MILK!

WHY DO CATS SLEEP ON THE FLOOR?

BECAUSE OF THE CAR-PET!

WHAT LOOKS LIKE HALF A CAT?

THE OTHER HALF!

WHY DO CATS MAKE GOOD STUNT DOUBLES?

THEY HAVE NINE LIVES!

WHAT PARTY GAME DO CATS LOVE?

MEW-SICAL CHAIRS!

HOW DO YOU SPELL MOUSETRAP WITH ONLY THREE LETTERS?

C-A-T

WHY DO PEOPLE LOVE CATS?

BECAUSE THEY ARE PURRFECT!

HOW DID THE CAT KNOW THEY HAD COVID?

BECAUSE THEY TESTED PAWS-ITIVE!

WHY DID THE CAT SLEEP UNDER THE CAR?

BECAUSE HE WANTED TO WAKE UP OILY!

WHAT DO YOU CALL A GREAT WHITE TERRORIZING A RESORT TOWN?

CLAWS!

DID YOU HEAR ABOUT THE CAT THAT ATE A BALL OF WOOL?

SHE HAD A LITTER OF MITTENS!

DID YOU HEAR THE CAT PIZZA JOKE?

NEVER MIND, IT WAS TOO CHEESY!

WHAT SHOULD YOU USE TO COMB A CAT?

A CATACOMB!

WHAT DO CATS LIKE TO EAT ON A HOT DAY?

MICE CREAM!

WHAT DID THE CAT SAY WHEN SHE WAS CONFUSED?

I'M PURR-PLEXED!

WHAT TYPE OF CATS PURR THE BEST?

PURR-SIANS!

WHAT HAPPENED WHEN A CAT
WENT TO THE FLEA CIRCUS?

SHE STOLE THE WHOLE SHOW!

IN WHAT KIND OF WEATHER IS
A VET AT THEIR BUSIEST?

WHEN IT'S RAINING CATS AND
DOGS!

WHAT DOES A CAT DO AFTER IT
WAKES UP IN THE MORNING?

IT GOES BACK TO
SLEEP!

STAY
PAWSITIVE!

CHAPTER 2: REVENGE OF THE MEWS

LOVE CATS

WHAT TYPE OF CAT LIVES UNDER THE SEA?

A PURR-MAID!

WHY CAN'T CATS PLAY POKER IN THE JUNGLE?

TOO MANY CHEETAHS!

BEFORE CHASING A MOUSE, WHAT DO CATS SAY?

LET US PREY!

LOVE CATS

WHAT BOOK DO CATS LOVE THE MOST?

THE PRINCESS AND THE PAW-PER!

WHEN IS IT BAD LUCK TO SEE A BLACK CAT?

WHEN YOU ARE A MOUSE!

WANNA HEAR A BAD CAT JOKE?

JUST KITTEN!

LOVE CATS

WHAT DO YOU CALL A CAT WHO GETS WHAT HE WANTS?

PURR-SUASIVE!

WHY DON'T CATS PLAY GO-FISH?

THEY GET TOO DISTRACTED BY THE FISH!!

WHAT IS A MOUSE'S LEAST FAVORITE SONG?

WHAT'S UP PUSSYCAT!

LOVE CATS

HOW DO CATS LIKE THEIR WATER?

PURR-IFIED!

WHAT GAMES DO CATS LIKE TO PLAY THE MOST WITH MICE?

CATCH!

WHAT KIND OF MUSICIAN DID THE CAT WANT TO BE?

A PURR-CUSSIONIST!

YOU LOVE CATS TOO?

THAT'S PAW-SOME!

LOVE CATS

WHAT DO CATS USE TO MIX CAKE BATTER?

A WHISKER!

WHAT DO YOU SAY WHEN YOUR CAT LEAVES THE HOUSE?

HAVE A MICE DAY!

WHAT BUTTON DO CATS ALWAYS PRESS ON THE REMOTE?

PAWS!

LOVE CATS

WHAT DO YOU CALL A CAT WHO
LIVES IN AN IGLOO?

AN ESKIMEW!

WHAT DID ONE FLEA SAY TO THE
OTHER?

SHALL WE TAKE THE CAT OR
WALK!

WHAT DO YOU CALL A CAT WITH
A SHORT HAIRCUT?

A BOB CAT!

LOVE CATS

WHO WEARS RED AND BRINGS CATNIP TO SLEEPING KITTENS?

SANTA CLAWS!

WHAT DID THE ALIEN SAY TO THE CAT?

TAKE ME TO YOUR LITTER!

WHO WAS THE MOST POWERFUL CAT IN CHINA?

CHAIRMAN MIAOW

LOVE CATS

WHAT MUSICAL DO ALL CATS LOVE?

THE SOUND OF MEW-SIC!

WHAT DID THE CAT SAY WHEN IT GOT SCRATCHED?

MEOWCH!

WHAT HAPPENED WHEN I DIDN'T LAUGH AT MY CAT'S JOKE?

HE TOOK IT PURR-SONALLY!

LOVE CATS

WHAT DO YOU GET WHEN YOU CROSS A CAT WITH A PARROT?

A CARROT!

WHAT DO YOU CALL A FLUFFY MALE CAT ASLEEP ON A BED?

A HIMALAYAN!

WHAT'S A CAT'S FAVORITE SHAKESPEARE QUOTE?

TABBY OR NOT TABBY? THAT IS THE QUESTION.

LOVE CATS

WITH THE RIGHT CATITUDE,

ANYTHING IS PAWSIBLE!

LOVE CATS

WHY COULDN'T THE OLD CAT SEE?

HE HAD CAT-ARACTS!

WHAT DOES A CAT HAVE THAT NO OTHER ANIMAL DOES?

KITTENS!

WHY DID THE CAT WEAR A DRESS?

SHE WAS FELINE FINE!

LOVE CATS

WHERE DO KITTENS GO ON A
SCHOOL TRIP?

TO THE MEWSEUM!

WHY DON'T CATS SHOP ONLINE?

THEY PREFER A CAT-ALOGUE!

WHAT WORD DO MILLENNIAL
CATS OVERUSE?

LITTER-ALLY!

LOVE CATS

WHAT DO CATS WEAR
TO PREVENT THEM
SMELLING BAD?

ANTI-PURR-SPIRANT!

HOW DO POLITE CATS
APOLOGISE?

PAW-DON ME! I'M
FURRY
SORRY!

LoVe CATS

WHAT SPORTS DO CATS PLAY AT
THE OLYMPICS?

HAIRBALL!

WHAT DO CATS READ IN
THE MORNING?

THE MEWSPAPER!

WHAT IS THE BEST MEDICATION
FOR CAT ALLERGIES?

AN ANTI-HISS-TAMINE!

LOVE CATS

WHY ARE CATS SCARED OF TREES?

BECAUSE OF THEIR BARK!

WHAT CAR DO CATS LOVE TO DRIVE?

A CAT-ILLAC!

WHAT DO YOU GET WHEN YOU CROSS A CHICK WITH AN ALLEY CAT?

A PEEPING TOM!

LOVE CATS

PAW-DON ME, BUT ARE YOU FUR REAL?!

LOVE CATS

WHAT SHOW DO CATS LOVE TO
WATCH ON TV?

THE EVENING MEWS!

WHY ARE CATS BETTER THAN
BABIES?

YOU ONLY HAVE TO CHANGE A
LITTER BOX ONCE A DAY!

WHAT MADE THE CAT UPGRADE
HER PHONE?

SHE WANTED PAWTRAIT
MODE!

LOVE CATS

WHY DO CATS NOT LAUGH AT JOKES?

THEY TAKE THINGS TOO LITTER-ALLY!

WHAT HAPPENS WHEN CATS FALL IN LOVE?

THEY GET MEOW-IED!

WHAT DID THE CAT SAY BEFORE THEIR FIGHT?

HOLD MY PURRSE!

LOVE CATS

WHAT DID THE CAT SAY AFTER A DISASTER?

THAT WAS CAT-ASTROPHIC!

HAVE YOU EVER SEEN A CATFISH?

NO. DO THEY USE RODS OR NETS?

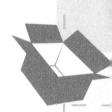

IF CARS RUN ON GAS, WHAT DO CATS RUN ON?

THEIR PAWS!

LOVE CATS

AM I AN OBSESSIVE
CAT PERSON?

THAT'S CERTAINLY
A PAW-SIBILITY!

LOVE CATS

WHAT DO YOU CALL A CAT THAT IS SCARED OF SMALL SPACES?

CLAWSTROPHOBIC!

WHY WAS THE PASSENGER ESCORTED OFF THE PLANE?

SHE LET THE CAT OUT OF THE BAG!

WHAT DID THE CAT SAY AFTER HEARING A FUNNY JOKE?

LMAO!

LOVE CATS

HOW DOES A CAT KEEP HIS
GARDEN TIDY?

WITH A LAWN MEOWER!

WHERE DO CATS WRITE DOWN
THEIR NOTES?

ON SCRATCH PAPER!

WHAT IS A CAT'S FAVORITE
MEXICAN DISH?

PURRITOS!

LOVE CATS

WHAT DO CATS DO AT THE END
OF A PLAY?

GIVE A ROUND OF A-PLAWS!

WHAT DO CATS DO AFTER
THEY FIGHT?

THEY HISS AND MAKE-UP!

WHAT DO CHRISTMAS AND
DESERT CATS HAVE IN COMMON?

SANDY CLAWS!

LoVe CATS

MEOW YOU DOIN'?

LOVE CATS

WHAT IS A CAT CAUGHT DOING A
CRIME CALLED?

A PURR-PETRATOR!

WHERE IS ONE PLACE THAT YOUR
CAT CAN SIT, BUT YOU CAN'T?

YOUR LAP!

WHAT DO YOU GET IF YOU CROSS
A CAT AND A BALL?

A FUR BALL!

LOVE CATS

WHAT MAGAZINE DO CATS PREFER?

GOOD MOUSEKEEPING!

A DUCK, A COW, AND A CAT GO OUT FOR DINNER, WHO HAD TO PAY?

THE DUCK, HE'S THE ONLY ONE WITH A BILL!

WHAT SUBJECT DO CATS LOVE AT SCHOOL?

MEWSIC!

LoVe CATS

WHERE DO INDEPENDENT CATS DECIDE TO LIVE?

CAT-A-LONIA!

WHERE DID THE CAT GO WHEN THEY LOST THEIR TAIL?

THE RE-TAIL STORE!

LoVe CATS

WHAT DID THE HAPPY CAT SAY?

I'M FELINE GOOD!

WHAT IS SMARTER THAN A TALKING CAT?

A SPELLING BEE!

WHAT HAPPENS WHEN A KITTEN TURNS ONE?

SHE HAS A PAW-TY!

LOVE CATS

WHAT COLOR DO CATS WEAR
WHEN THEY ARE FEELING GOOD?

PURR-PLE!

WHAT DO KITTENS WEAR?

DIA-PURRS!

HOW IS CAT FOOD SOLD?

PURR CAN!

LoVe CATS

YOU'RE PURRFECT JUST THE WAY YOU ARE!

LOVE CATS

WHY DO LEOPARDS NEVER WIN
HIDE-AND-SEEK?

THEY ARE ALWAYS SPOTTED!

WHAT DO CATS LOVE FOR
DESSERT?

CHOCOLATE MOUSE!

WHAT SONG DO CATS LIKE
TO SING?

THREE BLIND MICE!

LOVE CATS

WHAT COUNTRY HAS LOTS OF CATS AND DOGS?

PETSYLVANIA!

WHAT DO CATS DO WHEN THEY DO SOMETHING WRONG?

THEY A-PAW-LOGISE!

WHAT DO YOU CALL A CAT WITH 100 LEGS?

A CAT-ERPILLAR!

IF THERE WERE 5 CATS IN A BOAT AND 1 JUMPED OUT, HOW MANY REMAIN IN THE BOAT?

NONE, BECAUSE THEY WERE ALL COPYCATS!

LoVe CATS

WHAT HAPPENS IF YOU CROSS A
CAT WITH A SNOWMAN?

FROST-BITE!

WHY WAS THE CAT KICKED OUT
OF THE GAME?

THE REF THOUGHT SHE WAS A
CHEETAH!

WHAT DID SPOCK SAY TO HIS
CAT?

LIVE LONG AND
PAW-SPER!

LOVE CATS

WHY DID THE CAT INVEST IN THE STOCK MARKET?

SHE THOUGHT IT WAS A GREAT OP-PAW-TUNITY!

WHAT DOES A CAT SAY WHEN IT GETS SCARED?

THAT FREAKS MEOWT!

WHERE DOES A CAT ORDER THEIR CLOTHES FROM?

FROM A CAT-ALOG!

LOVE CATS

SO FUR, SO GOOD!

LOVE CATS

WHAT TYPE OF CATS DO BAKERS OWN?

PURE-BREADS!

WHY DO CATS HAVE NICE BREATH?

BECAUSE THEY USE MOUSEWASH

WHAT DO YOU CALL A CAT TEACHER?

A PURR-FESSOR!

LoVe CATS

HOW DO LIONS GREET
PEOPLE?

PLEASED TO EAT YOU!

WHAT POPSTAR DO ALL CATS
LOVE?

KITTY PERRY!

WHAT BIRDS DO CATS LOVE?

E-MEWS!

LOVE CATS

WHY DIDN'T ANYONE TRUST THE TIGER?

THEY THOUGHT IT WAS A LION!

WHY ARE CATS SUCH GREAT SINGERS?

BECAUSE THEY ARE VERY MEWSICAL!

HOW DO CATS EXPRESS THEIR LOVE?

IN HOLY CATRIMONY!

LOVE CATS

AS GOOD AS MEW!

DID YOU HEAR ABOUT THE CAT WHO DRANK 10 BOWLS OF WATER?

HE SET A NEW LAP RECORD!

WHAT HAPPENED TO THE BAD VET?

HE WAS SUED FOR MEOW-PRACTICE!

WHY DO CATS MAKE SUCH GREAT MODELS?

BECAUSE THEY ROCK THE CATWALK!

LoVe CATS

DOGS CAN'T
OPERATE AN MRI
MACHINE...

BUT CATSCAN!

A CATTY FURWELL!

Made in the USA
Middletown, DE
30 November 2022